Reading Primary Literature
A Practical Guide to Evaluating Research Articles in Biology

Christopher M. Gillen

Kenyon College

PEARSON

Benjamin
Cummings

San Francisco   Boston   New York
Cape Town   Hong Kong   London   Madrid   Mexico City
Montreal   Munich   Paris   Singapore   Sydney   Tokyo   Toronto

Development Manager: Claire Alexander
Acquisitions Editor: Susan Winslow
Assistant Editor: Mercedes Grandin
Executive Marketing Manager: Lauren Harp
Managing Editor: Deborah Cogan
Production Supervisor: Shannon Tozier
Project Management, Composition, and Illustrations: Black Dot Group
Manufacturing Manager: Stacey Weinberger
Text Design: Black Dot Group
Cover Design: Seventeenth Street Studios and Marilyn Perry
Text and Cover Printer: RR Donnelley
Cover Photo: Richard Megna/Fundamental Photographs

Reviewers: Shivanthi Anandan *Drexel University,* Christine Broussard *University of La Verne,* Leslie Brown *Goucher College,* Michael Buratovich *Spring Arbor University,* Cynthia Cooper *Truman State University,* Marya Czech *Lourdes College,* David Daleke *Indiana University,* Dana M. Garcia *Texas State University,* Mike Geusz *Bowling Green State University,* Kathy M. Gillen *Kenyon College,* Robert Gregerson *Lyon College,* Mark Hens *University of North Carolina at Greensboro,* Deborah Hettinger *Texas Lutheran University,* Cindy Klevickis *James Madison University,* Todd Kostman *University of Wisconsin - Oshkosh,* Jani Lewis *SUNY Geneseo,* Jackie Miller *Ohio State University,* Brad Stith *University of Colorado - Denver,* Louise Wootton *Georgian Court University,* Jenny Dellapietro *Georgian Court University (student),* Christy John *Georgian Court University (student)*

ISBN-13: 978-08053-4599-5
ISBN-10: 0-8053-4599-X

Contents

Section 1: Introduction to the Booklet   1
    What Are Primary Research Articles?   1
    Why Read the Primary Literature?   2
    How to Use This Booklet   2

Section 2: Finding Research Articles   3
    Window-Shopping: Browsing Journals   3
    Needle in a Haystack: Searching Databases   5
    Section 2 Exercises   6

Section 3: The Anatomy of a Paper   7
    Formatting Matters   7
    Citation   8
        Authors: The Research Team   9
        Publication Dates: Peer Review   10
    Abstract   12
    Acknowledgments   13
    References   13
    The Extended Research Team   14
    Section 3 Exercises   14

Section 4: The Introduction   15
    Understanding the Jargon   15
    Observations, Explanations, Experiments   17
    Science as a Cyclical Process   19
    Section 4 Exercises   20

Section 5: The Materials and Methods   20
    Preliminary Work and Approvals   21
    Nuts and Bolts: Experimental Details   21
        Dependent Variables   22
        Independent Variables   22
        Controlled Variables   22
        Controls   23

Reproducibility and Repeatability   24

The Big Picture: Experimental Design   24

    Correlative Studies: Patterns and Connections   25

    Correlative Studies: Challenges and Limitations   25

    Causative Studies: Between-Groups Design   26

    Causative Studies: Repeated-Measures Design   26

    Model Systems   26

    Evaluating Experimental Design   27

Section 5 Exercises   28

Section 6: The Results   29

Dealing with Variability: Statistics   29

    Descriptive Statistics: Central Tendency and Variability   30

    Inferential Statistics: From a Sample to a Population   31

    Statistical Tests: Null and Alternative Hypotheses   32

    Positive Results   33

    Negative Results   33

    Biological Relevance   34

Visualizing Results: Tables and Graphs   34

    Graphs   35

    Evaluating Data   36

Section 6 Exercises   37

Section 7: The Discussion   38

Interpretation: Finding Meaning   38

Connections: Relationship to Other Work   39

Explanations and Implications   40

Section 7 Exercises   40

Section 8: Putting It All Together   41

Resources for Students and Educators   42

Websites   42

Books   42

Articles About Reading Papers   43

Example Research Articles   43

Section 1: Introduction to the Booklet

Primary research articles are an excellent resource for students of biology. Reading papers opens a doorway into the world of scientific research. As you begin reading articles, you will be challenged to think critically, apply your knowledge, and use the scientific method. The purpose of this booklet is to guide you through this process. It describes the tools and strategies you'll need to begin reading articles.

WHAT ARE PRIMARY RESEARCH ARTICLES?

Primary research articles, also called **research papers** or **primary literature**, are the official documents that scientists use to communicate their research to each other. Research papers describe original findings, including methodology and results. In contrast, documents that synthesize, summarize, or evaluate primary literature are termed **secondary** sources. Common secondary sources include magazine articles, dictionaries, textbooks, and websites. Magazines written for the general public, such as *Discover* and *Scientific American*, publish only secondary articles. Some publications, such as the scientific journals *Science* and *Nature*, publish a mixture of primary research papers and secondary reports. Primary papers are always written by scientists, while secondary reports may be written by scientists, journalists, or others. In practice, you'll need to look at each source carefully to determine if it is primary or secondary. Primary sources include a detailed description of the methods and results. They are the first report of original research findings and are written by the scientists who performed the work. This book focuses on primary research articles.

You've probably spent hours reading science textbooks. They describe accepted scientific facts and concepts, and they are written towards a student audience. In contrast, research articles address areas of emerging knowledge or controversy, and they are written with professional scientists as the intended audience. Research articles represent science in process, while textbooks describe the outcome of that process. Reading research articles requires different strategies than reading textbooks, and you will encounter new challenges as you begin reading them. This booklet will give you the tools to overcome the challenges.

WHY READ THE PRIMARY LITERATURE?

Doing science is a powerful way to learn it. In your laboratory classes, you begin participating in science by performing key experiments and techniques. Reading research articles is another way to become involved in the scientific process, because evaluating research articles is a central activity of practicing scientists. Think of research papers as a doorway into the scientific world. They present the chance to apply material that you've learned through reading textbooks and listening to lectures. They challenge you to think along with scientists as they tackle research problems. They serve as examples for your own scientific writing. And they encourage you to critically analyze new scientific ideas.

Try to approach reading research articles as a challenge rather than a chore. While the primary literature may appear dry, under the surface you will find drama and controversy. Research scientists constantly face mysteries because they work at the edge of our knowledge. So research articles can be like detective novels, in which scientists carefully gather the clues and evidence needed to solve scientific problems. Further, like a good detective novel, the course of science often has entertaining twists and surprises. Finally, the research literature reflects upon the scientists themselves. It documents how their tools, priorities, and practices change over time and how they cooperate and compete with each other. Recognize the personal side of science; it will add useful context to the research articles you read.

Learning to read research articles has obvious benefits if you plan to pursue a research career in biology. But the brief exposure to the primary literature afforded by this booklet will be beneficial even if you never again read a primary literature article. As a child, I took up the trumpet and learned to play the "Star Wars Theme" loud enough to drive our Irish Setter under the kitchen table. However, I never became especially skilled, and I can't play a note today. Yet my battles with the trumpet continue to enrich my adult life by enhancing my appreciation and understanding of music. In the same way, learning to read primary literature opens the door towards comprehending and evaluating all sorts of scientific information. Learn to read research articles and you will become a more confident and effective judge of scientific information, a remarkably useful skill in today's world.

HOW TO USE THIS BOOKLET

Learning to read primary research articles is a lot like learning other demanding activities. For example, imagine that you've been handed a fishing rod and a tackle box. Without any advice, trying to catch fish using these tools will be hard. Some tips and advice from an expert will greatly ease your way. But instruction alone won't make you a competent angler. You'll need to go stand by the water and practice baiting a hook, casting a line, and landing a fish. So it is with reading research articles; both *instruction* and *practice* are needed.

This booklet is the instruction manual you'll need to quickly become a talented reader of research articles. The sections cover how to find articles, the structure of research articles, and the four main parts of an article: the Introduction, Materials and Methods, Results, and Discussion. In addition to studying this booklet, you'll also need to struggle with research articles yourself. The end-of-section exercises will prompt that practice; they ask you to critically read a paper by applying the section's advice. Depending on your course and instructor, you might choose your own article using the instructions in section 2 or your instructor might assign one.

As you begin your journey into the primary literature of biology, there will inevitably be obstacles and frustrations. But I hope you will also find satisfaction in overcoming the challenges and participating in the process of science.

Section 2: *Finding Research Articles*

The major journals in biomedicine now publish online. More than a million scientific articles are available free on the Internet, and many more can be accessed for a fee. Along with this availability comes challenges. Scientists need to find relevant information amidst a mountain of data and then intelligently analyze the information. This section describes the first step: locating and accessing research articles. The details will be specific to your institution and subdiscipline, so we will focus on general strategies and free online databases. You should also learn about the specific resources available on your campus.

The strategies you employ will depend on the purpose of your search. Are you trying to develop a topic for a research paper? Scanning the table of contents of a prestigious journal might give you some ideas about current hot research areas. You might also look at secondary sources such as textbooks and magazines for ideas. If you've already selected a general topic area, but need to find articles within that topic, then you might decide to search databases of research articles. Or perhaps you've already found an interesting article and now need to read some related articles to put it in context. In this case, you might look at the sources it cites and also search databases.

WINDOW-SHOPPING: BROWSING JOURNALS

Suppose you wish to browse journals to develop topic ideas. Where can you find journals? One place is your school's library, which has hard copies of many journals. Having the paper journal in your hands can be particularly useful when you are browsing for interesting topics. Of course, many journals are also available online. If you already know which journal you want to browse, a simple strategy is to locate its homepage with an Internet search engine. Online journals have straightforward interfaces that allow you to browse or search for articles.

Another way to access online journals is through a website that catalogs and organizes them. For example, you will find many important journals in biomedicine at the Highwire Press site hosted by Stanford University Libraries (www.highwire.org). Excellent instructions for using the site are available on its homepage. You can see a list of journals, choose one that matches your interests, and browse the tables of contents of recent issues. For many journals, access to the most recently published articles requires a subscription, with free access available about a year after publication. A useful feature of the Highwire site is a listing of journals with free online access.

Almost 1000 scientific journals are hosted on Highwire. How can you decide which journals are the most relevant to your topic? Which are the most reliable? Which are the most prestigious? One strategy is to look in the references section of your class textbook to see which journals are cited; these are likely to be relevant to your course and highly regarded. As you begin to find research articles, you can also check their References Cited sections; again, the journals that are regularly cited are the most useful and prestigious. Journal rankings also exist. One widely used measure, the **impact factor**, measures how many times the articles published in a journal are cited by other articles. Finally, you can ask your course instructor or librarian. Widely read and cited journals that publish research in biology include: *Science, Nature, Cell, Development, Genetics, Proceedings of the National Academies of Science (PNAS), Journal of Biological Chemistry, Journal of Clinical Investigation, Journal of Experimental Biology, American Journal of Physiology, Neuron, Journal of Bacteriology,* and *Public Library of Science (PLoS) Biology.* This is a partial list; there are many other outstanding journals.

Another useful website is BioMed Central (www.biomedcentral.com), which publishes more than 150 journals, including general titles such as *BMC Biology* and *Journal of Biology* and specialized titles such as *BMC Physiology* and *BMC Microbiology.* Articles published in BioMed Central are **open-access**, meaning that they can be freely accessed and distributed. You can search all of the BioMed Central journals or browse particular titles.

Online articles are usually available in two formats: full-text and PDF. PDF files, which are viewable using the Adobe Reader®, faithfully represent the article as it appears in the print journal. Access the PDF version if you wish to print the article. In contrast, the full-text version of an article does not attempt to represent the actual printed article; instead full-text versions use html format and therefore may include special features not available in the printed article. For example, links may enable you to navigate easily throughout the article, to access supporting documents such as supplemental data, and to go to full-text versions of other articles.

Suppose you have chosen to work with a particular article. The html version of your article can be an entry point into an interconnected web of references. You may find links to other articles, including those by the same authors, those that your article cites, and those that cite your article. In contrast to the printed version of an article, the html version can be updated, so that links can be included to sources that were published after the original paper. For example, you can't identify papers that refer to your article by looking at the printed version, but the html version may contain this information. Locating such sources can be valuable since they may offer commentary on your article. The *Science Citation Index*, which is available at many institutions, is another tool that enables you to identify sources that cite a particular article.

NEEDLE IN A HAYSTACK: SEARCHING DATABASES

Suppose you have developed a research topic and need to find relevant primary sources. Or maybe you have found a single journal article and need to find additional articles on the same topic. In both cases, searching a research article database will be an effective approach. Several databases may be available on your campus; choose the one best suited to your topic. Although details will vary slightly from one to the next, the general principles will be the same, and most databases contain helpful instructions to get you started.

As an example, we'll discuss the freely available PUBMED site, which is part of an interconnected collection of databases operated by the National Center for Biotechnology Information (NCBI, www.ncbi.nlm.nih.gov). PUBMED allows users to search articles in almost 5,000 journals in medicine and related fields. In total, over 15 million citations are included. Given the huge number of citations in PUBMED, separating useful articles from all of the rest can be tricky. Good searches will be *comprehensive*, meaning they will return all or most of the articles on a particular topic, and will also be well *focused*, meaning they will return a reasonable number of articles with few irrelevant articles.

The choice of **search terms** is obviously crucial to an effective search. You can find search terms on the first page of research articles; look for a list of terms below the Abstract. You might also pick up useful terms in secondary sources or by browsing article titles. Scientists often use specialized words with precise meanings, so it also helps to know some of the scientific vocabulary. For example, while the general public says "heart attack," a scientist may say "sudden cardiac death," "myocardial infarction," "heart failure," "cardiac ischemia," or "ventricular fibrillation," with each of these phrases having a somewhat different meaning. Searches using different terms will return different sets of articles. Knowing exactly which terms to use can be difficult to determine, and some trial and error may be needed. Don't be afraid to start searching with a term that might be imperfect. Searches are free and fast, and better search terms can often be gleaned from the citations returned by an initial search.

Because scientists may use various terms for the same concept, many databases include a **controlled subject vocabulary**. In PUBMED, these terms are called the Medical Subject Headings (MeSH). You can find MeSH words by searching the MeSH database on the NCBI site. For example, searching for "cardiac ischemia" returns two MeSH terms: "myocardial ischemia" and "coronary arteriosclerosis." The term that best matches your interest can be used as a search term, leading to a comprehensive and well-focused search.

Once you've identified some useful search terms, a good strategy is to start with general searches and then try to focus. Preliminary searches may yield an unmanageable number of articles. For example, PUBMED returns about 250,000 articles for the search term "hypertension" and 200,000 articles for "diet." Combining terms using AND will focus the search. About 10,000 articles are returned for "diet AND hypertension," a lot less than either term alone but still probably too many to sift through. The search can be further narrowed using the LIMIT function, which enables you to select features such as publication date range, language, subject (animal or human), subject age, and online availability of the full-text article. You can also restrict your search to only article titles or abstracts to narrow the search further.

Using the operator OR between terms will return all the citations that contain either term and thus can be useful for generating a comprehensive citation list. For example, if you wish to make a complete search about athletics, you might combine "athletics" with "sports" using OR. Searching "athletics OR sports" will return more articles than using either term alone. The NOT operator is also handy. Placing NOT before a search term eliminates all articles containing the term, thereby reducing the number of articles returned. Suppose you find that a major portion of the literature on sports and athletics deals with badminton, a sport that does not interest you. NOT could eliminate articles about badminton, thus returning a more reasonable total number of articles.

Searches that return between 10 and 100 articles are good starting points. You can scan the titles for articles that match your interest. Both Highwire and PUBMED mark free access articles with special icons, so you can easily identify them. However, be careful not to let free availability be a major search criterion. You may have access to many articles not listed in these databases as free. Your library may subscribe to the journal either in paper or online, or you may be able to obtain the article through an interlibrary loan. Check with a librarian at your institution for more information.

SECTION 2 EXERCISES

These exercises will help you locate and access research articles:

1. Visit your library or access an online database. Identify several journals in your area of study that publish primary research articles. Browse the table of contents of these journals and scan some of the articles. List two or three differences among the journals you've found.

2. Locate the journals *Nature* (www.nature.com) and *Science* (www .sciencemag.org), again either online or at the library. Browse through an issue of one of these journals and identify primary and secondary articles. Write down the titles, authors, journal, year, volume, and page numbers of three primary and three secondary articles.

3. Develop a list of three research topics that interest you, using your textbook, popular magazine articles, Internet news sites, and other secondary sources.

4. Develop a list of three current research topics by browsing through the table of contents of recent journal issues. Look for topics that are explored in several recent articles.

5. Choose one of the research topics from question three or four and develop a list of five search terms that could be used to search for research articles on the topic.

6. Using an appropriate database, identify five primary research articles on your topic.

7. Pick one of the articles from question six. Develop a list of at least five research articles that would help you understand the chosen article. Look for articles cited by the chosen article, articles that cite it, and other articles by the same authors. Also, search appropriate databases to find additional related articles.

Section 3: The Anatomy of a Paper

Most biology research papers contain the following sections: Citation, Abstract, Introduction, Materials and Methods, Results, Discussion, Acknowledgments, and References. In this section, we first consider the ways that you can use the format of papers to read efficiently and critically. We then discuss the Citation, Abstract, Acknowledgments and References sections. Subsequent sections will be devoted to the Introduction, Materials and Methods, Results, and Discussion.

FORMATTING MATTERS

Research articles share a common **format**; material is presented in discrete sections arranged in a particular order. For instance, the Materials and Methods section, which describes exactly how the work was done, usually precedes the Results section, which portrays the data. This formatting is not only convenient for readers and writers; it also enables research to be judged according to the standards of the scientific community.

The format of research papers can help you maintain a critical stance. Because each aspect of the study is described in a separate section, you can independently assess different aspects of a study. For example, original data are presented entirely in the Results, while interpretation of data is mainly confined to the Discussion. You can exploit this separation by closely analyzing the data in the Results before considering interpretations in the Discussion.

The format of papers also allows you to quickly access information. To make the most of this, try to approach a paper with specific objectives. You may want to use the Introduction as background information about a new topic. You may focus on the Materials and Methods if you wish to find techniques to use in your own research project. You may want to compare the study's Results with those of another study. Or you may be interested in how a famous scientist synthesizes new research in the Discussion. Make yourself familiar with the format of papers; it will allow you to go directly to the desired information.

Journals vary in their formatting. Sometimes the Materials and Methods are at the end of the article rather than following the Introduction. Sometimes the Results and Discussion are combined into a single section. Sometimes, most notably in the very influential *Nature* and *Science*, the text is not divided into separate sections. However, if you are familiar with the standard format of papers, you can adjust to these modified formats. Look for writing that corresponds to each of the sections of a standard article.

The format of papers is not only helpful to readers; it may also impact the scientific process. Scientists need to communicate their findings effectively in research articles, so they may anticipate the paper they plan to write while they are collecting data. In this way, the demands placed on authors by the format of papers can influence the way they conduct their studies. This influence is overwhelmingly positive, because the format of papers is consistent with the methodological standards of the scientific community. If you are conducting independent research, you may find it useful to think about how you will present your work before you perform your studies. Will you be able to make a convincing case to other scientists?

CITATION

Basic **citation** information is given at the top of an article's first page: the title, authors, institutional affiliations, journal, volume, pages, and publication date (Figure 1). Don't skip this information; it can be surprisingly useful. The journal name, volume, and page numbers form a unique "address" and can be used to identify a particular article. You can often find the journal's **publisher** on the first page. Some journals are published by scientific societies, for example the American Physiological Society or the American Society of Microbiologists. Others are produced by commercial publishers. While journals produced by societies and companies can both be reliable, it helps to know what organization is behind the journal. Also scrutinize the **title**, which usually includes the species studied, the experimental approach, and perhaps a brief indication of the results obtained. Reading article

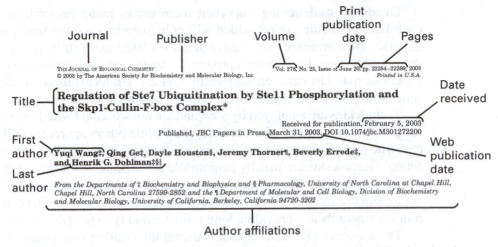

FIGURE 1. The header of a scientific paper. In this example, a Web publication date is given rather than a paper acceptance date. Adapted with permission from the American Society for Biochemistry and Molecular Biology.

titles carefully can save you time; you can often decide whether you wish to read any further.

Authors: The Research Team

The stereotype of the lonely scientist working in the solitary confinement of a laboratory stands in direct contrast to the collaborative, interdisciplinary world of modern science. Most modern research articles have multiple authors, reflecting this collaborative model. Let's look at the personnel in a typical research group and explore how they are represented in an author list.

Scientists work in diverse research groups that ordinarily include people of different ages, backgrounds, and educations. The boss is the **principal investigator (PI)**, an established scientist who usually has a PhD or MD. PIs determine research priorities, write grants, hire personnel, present findings at conferences, convene lab meetings, and revise manuscripts. They are ultimately responsible for the work done in their lab. Research groups contain other scientists who have finished their education. **Postdoctoral fellows** ("post-docs" for short) have recently received a PhD or MD, but have not yet established their own research program. They are experienced, free from other responsibilities, highly motivated, and often the most productive members of a research group. Groups may also include **senior research scientists** who are well past the post-doc portion of their career and have a long-term position. Finally, **collaborators** may join a research group for a particular project. Collaborators may come from across the hall or from across the globe, and many laboratory groups are distinctly multinational.

Graduate students are important members of many research groups. They each have a specific project which will culminate in a written thesis and an oral defense. Their research both contributes to science and fulfills a requirement of their degree programs. Master's programs usually last one or two years while PhD programs may last between four and six years. **Undergraduate** students sometimes work in labs during the summer or part time during the school year.

Technicians are employed by a lab and are not working towards a degree. Some are permanent members of a research group while others are recent college graduates who plan to work for a year or two before applying to graduate or professional school. Technicians are usually responsible for aspects of the day-to-day work of the lab. They perform experiments, order supplies, analyze data, and train students. An experienced technician can be a central member of a lab group, keeping the lab running smoothly and providing long-term continuity to the lab's workings.

The sequence of authors contains useful information (see Figure 1). The **first author** is usually the scientist who did the most work on a project, often a senior scientist, post-doc, or graduate student. The PI is often listed as the **last author** and is also sometimes called the **senior author**. The first and last authors get a major portion of the credit for the study. **Middle authors** may have contributed in any number of ways, for example, by providing technical help or by reading and editing the manuscript. They get considerably less credit than first and last authors. If you wish to track down similar studies, focus your attention on the first and last authors, who are most likely to have done additional work on the topic.

Who is included as an author? Scientific ethics require that only those who have made an intellectual contribution to the work be listed. It is unethical to omit someone who has significantly contributed to a project or to include someone who has not had a substantive role. In the end, each author is responsible for the content of the paper. When technicians or undergraduates have made an intellectual contribution to the project, they are listed as authors. Otherwise, they might be thanked in the Acknowledgments.

Consider the institutional affiliations of the authors. Are all of the authors from the same institution or is this a multi-institutional collaboration? What sorts of institutions are involved? Major research universities? Drug manufacturers? Liberal arts colleges? Are the authors associated with basic science departments (i.e., Cell Biology, Biochemistry, Physiology) or are they associated with clinical departments (i.e., Internal Medicine, Nephrology, Oncology)? The institutional affiliations can tell you about the authors' perspectives.

Publication Dates: Peer Review
On the first page of an article, you may find several dates, including the date the article was received by the journal, the date it was accepted for publication, and the print publication date (see Figure 1). Articles are sometimes posted on the Internet shortly after acceptance, and in such cases the date of first Internet publi-

cation may be given rather than the acceptance date. Why are there delays between receipt, acceptance, and publication? What happens in these interims? Let's look at the process of drafting, submitting, and revising a manuscript.

One scientist often writes a first draft of a research paper. After this initial effort, however, the process is usually distinctly collaborative. The draft will typically be read by several members of a research group, often resulting in substantial revisions. The manuscript may also be read by scientists outside the immediate research group, who can provide an objective perspective. After this initial "friendly" review, a manuscript may be ready to be sent to a journal. Choosing the appropriate journal is an important decision for authors. Authors seek to publish their work in prestigious, widely read journals. However, the review process can be lengthy, so it is risky to send an article to a top-notch journal where acceptance may be uncertain.

Submitted articles are first considered by an editor who assesses whether the manuscript is within the scope of the journal. If so, the editor will send it out to two or more anonymous reviewers. This process is called **peer review,** because the reviewers are the authors' peers: other research scientists with expertise in the study's topic. They critically read the manuscript and inform the editor of its suitability for publication. They may also be asked to rate the priority or importance of the manuscript. Reviewers also write a set of comments for the authors; these will be essential to the authors if they are asked to revise and resubmit. The final decision about publication is in the hands of the editor. The editor may simply reject the manuscript, accept it without revisions, ask for minor revisions, or require major issues to be addressed before resubmission.

Although you will not find any direct evidence of the peer review process in most papers, remember that each primary research article has been evaluated by other scientists before publication. One clue to the peer review process is the delay between submission and acceptance (or Internet publication) dates. If the article was accepted shortly after submission, it could mean that the reviewers examined it carefully and found it flawless. Or they might have looked at it quickly and missed an important issue. If there was a long delay, the authors might have been asked to make substantial revisions, perhaps even to supply additional data. On the other hand, a reviewer might simply have been late in submitting comments. Take note of the length of the delay between submission and acceptance, but don't put too much emphasis on it.

Once a manuscript is accepted, it will still be some time before the article is finally printed. Before publication in print, authors receive a formatted version of the article. They can respond to editorial changes, check for small errors, and answer questions from the publisher. Because the review and publication process can be lengthy, scientists find it helpful when the submission, acceptance, and publication dates are printed on the paper. Scientists get credit by publishing *original* findings. When multiple groups publish on the same topic, submission and acceptance dates can help resolve disagreements about who published first.

You can use these dates to help understand what the authors knew when they submitted an article. For example, an article submitted in October 2002 and published August 2003 could not reasonably be expected to consider information that was published in June 2003.

Peer review is a good way of evaluating the scientific value of papers before they are published. Errors are corrected, interpretations are refined, and explanations are deepened. Work that fails to meet basic standards isn't published. But peer review isn't perfect. Mistakes sometimes slip past reviewers, so don't be surprised if you find something in a paper that might be incorrect. Also, peer review isn't designed to uncover scientific fraud. In the rare cases where scientists intentionally misrepresent their work, peer reviewers are usually not in a position to detect the fraud. The system thus relies on the honesty of authors, and breaching this trust is considered to be an ethical lapse of the highest order. Fortunately, fraud is often exposed through other mechanisms, either by whistleblowers who have firsthand knowledge of the misconduct or as a consequence of other scientists failing to replicate key findings.

ABSTRACT

Abstracts are succinct summaries of research papers. They usually include statements of the study's purpose, experimental approach, key results, and conclusions. Each of the sections of a scientific paper is condensed into a few sentences in the Abstract. They are typically limited to less than 250 words, so each word must be carefully chosen.

Apart from the title, Abstracts are the most widely distributed portion of papers. They are freely available in online databases. Take the time to read the Abstract closely. It will introduce you to the study's core methods, findings, and conclusions, and help focus your further reading. Some Abstracts will be difficult to read. When an entire research study is condensed into a single paragraph, the writing must become quite dense. In some cases, it might be best to skim the Abstract and proceed to the other sections, where you will find more explanation. Don't quit reading an article just because the Abstract is too difficult. Give the rest of the paper a chance. Finally, resist the temptation to use the Abstract as a substitute for reading the full article. You won't find enough detail to make an informed judgment. Scientists don't cite an article solely based on the Abstract.

When scientists attend meetings, they frequently present their findings in short oral sessions or as posters. Such presentations are often accompanied by an Abstract, which is distributed to meeting attendees and sometimes published in a special journal issue. These Abstracts are similar to those that accompany a full-text scientific paper. But they are not supported by full-text papers, and they do not always receive critical peer review by other scientists. Thus, meeting abstracts may be less reliable documents than Abstracts of full-length papers. Much of the work presented at meetings will eventually be incorporated into peer-reviewed research articles, and meetings are an important way for scientists to get feedback on their work prior to publication.

ACKNOWLEDGMENTS

In the **Acknowledgments**, authors thank the people or institutions that have contributed to the work. Scientists acknowledge those who have given valuable feedback, either by reading a draft of the manuscript or by commenting on a preliminary presentation of the work. You can sometimes get a good sense for the pre-publication feedback that scientists received by seeing who they thank in the Acknowledgments. Authors may also acknowledge technical assistance and gifts of equipment, supplies, or reagents.

Research funding sources are noted in the Acknowledgments. Numerous sources of money are available to scientists, including the home institution, government agencies such as the National Science Foundation and the National Institutes of Health, industry groups such as pharmaceutical companies, and private research foundations such as the American Heart Association. Scientists apply for funding through **grant applications** that describe their past accomplishments and the proposed studies. These applications are evaluated by panels of scientists. Check the Acknowledgments to see how a study was funded. Since competition for grant monies can be extraordinarily competitive, funded projects have passed a rigorous peer review. Consider also whether the funding source could bias outcomes. Would you feel differently about a study funded by a pharmaceutical company compared to one funded by the government? Perhaps it would depend on the purpose of the research? Finally, post-docs and graduate students may receive fellowships to fund their studies. When these are noted in the Acknowledgments, it can help you identify which authors are students and post-docs.

Some journals ask authors to disclose possible conflicts of interest, usually in the Acknowledgments or in a separate statement at the end of the article. For example, scientists might have a financial interest in a company whose business is related to the study. Check to see if any of the authors have a direct financial stake in the outcome of the study; this might influence the way you evaluate the article.

REFERENCES

The **References** section is sometimes called the **References Cited** or **Literature Cited**. It includes only those articles cited in the text of the paper. By citing other studies, scientists acknowledge the work of others and position their own work within a larger body of scientific literature.

The References can be an excellent source for finding further reading on a topic. You may wish to analyze the kind of sources used in a paper. Have the authors previously published on this topic? Do they mainly cite their own works? Have the authors considered other recent studies? Have they read the older, classic literature on a topic? Have they considered the work of scientists outside their immediate field? Answers to some of these questions may be found with a quick look at the References, and if you wish to pursue the matter further you can read some of the cited articles.

THE EXTENDED RESEARCH TEAM

We have seen in this section that science is very much a team activity. The research team extends even beyond the list of authors to include other scientists from within and outside a research group. Members of a research team who are not authors often give feedback by reading drafts of the manuscript. They may also share opinions during **lab meetings**, which are regular meetings of research groups. Results and interpretations are usually given a rigorous challenge at these meetings; scientists evaluate their own findings critically before sharing them with other research groups.

Scientists outside the research group contribute to the work by reviewing manuscripts, assessing grant proposals, and offering technical help. They also comment on conference presentations and **research seminars**. Academic departments regularly invite speakers, often from outside their own institution, to present seminars. Speakers present their new findings and often receive questions and useful feedback. The audience learns about new research, often before it is published. Keep these inputs from other scientists in mind when reading a paper. By the time a paper has been published, the opinions of many scientists have been incorporated.

SECTION 3 EXERCISES

Using a research article as an example, complete the following exercises:

1. In one or two sentences, restate the title of the paper in a way that would be understandable to a member of the general public without a scientific background.

2. Who are the authors of the paper? What kind of institutions are they from? What kind of departments are they in? Do the institutional or departmental affiliations of the authors offer any insight into their perspective or possible biases? Can you identify the PI? Are any of the authors students?

3. When was the paper published? How long were the delays between submission and acceptance and publication?

4. Read the paper's Abstract. Summarize the main point of the study in two or three sentences.

5. Can you determine how the study was funded? If so, does the source of funding influence your opinion of the work?

6. Were any other scientists consulted in this project? Did the authors get feedback from other scientists prior to publication?

7. Examine the References. Do the authors cite themselves? Are some other authors cited frequently? Are recent works cited? Do the authors cite any older papers to provide an historical perspective? Do you see any sources that might help you understand the paper better?

Section 4: The Introduction

The Introduction contains background information and a description of the study's purpose. Authors describe a research problem, explain prior work, and indicate where controversy exists. They describe why their work is important and how it seeks to extend knowledge. You can use the Introduction to learn about previous studies in a research field and to understand the study's purpose.

UNDERSTANDING THE JARGON

Suppose you encounter an Introduction that is littered with unfamiliar technical language. It helps to know that scientists have valid reasons for employing specialized terminology. Scientific words or phrases can condense a large body of shared knowledge. For example, when cell biologists say "tyrosine kinase," they mean "a member of a class of enzymes that catalyzes the addition of a phosphate group to the amino acid tyrosine in certain proteins thereby affecting their function." Writing this every time would be cumbersome, so the technical language serves an important role. Taking the time to learn the specialized vocabulary may be time-consuming, but it's a necessity if you hope to appreciate the paper's scientific concepts.

To comprehend a paper's specialized terminology you may need to consult additional sources. Secondary sources, including textbooks, review articles, websites, and dictionaries, are useful tools for understanding scientific terminology and concepts. Some secondary sources are written specifically for nonscientists, and are easier to understand than research articles. However, because secondary sources are so varied, it's necessary to carefully evaluate the credibility of each source. Also, secondary sources must never substitute for careful reading of primary research papers. Scientists always consult primary sources on questions of central importance to their own work.

To master the terminology in a paper, note the most commonly used technical terms in the Introduction and then find definitions for them, using a biological, scientific, or medical dictionary. Such dictionaries can be found online and in the reference section of libraries. While looking for challenging terminology, pay particular attention to abbreviations and acronyms. These are often used extensively and can make an article seem incomprehensible. Abbreviations are sometimes defined in a list on the article's first page. Take the time to become familiar with each abbreviation.

Defining terms is a good start, but to fully understand the concept behind each term you may need to go beyond dictionaries and consult other sources. Books, including textbooks, can be a good tool. You probably know that as knowledge in biology has grown, textbooks have lengthened accordingly. Fortunately, using texts to understand the primary literature does not require a cover-to-cover read. Instead, you can identify topics in the table of contents or index, and read only the relevant sections. Encyclopedias and magazine articles can be used in similar fashion.

Review articles offer more specialized and focused background reading. They are often found in the same journals that publish primary research articles, but their focus is summarizing and synthesizing the findings of many studies rather than presenting new results. Reviews are written as communications to practicing scientists, and thus may be more difficult to understand than textbooks or magazine articles. However, they can provide an authoritative overview of a research field and usually have comprehensive references lists that can be a good source of further reading.

Information on the Internet can be both current and convenient to access. However, the quality of Internet sites is variable; some are trustworthy, others are not. Thus, evaluating the reliability of Internet sites is essential. Here are six elements that should be considered when evaluating websites:

1. Author. Who is the source of the information? Is there a single author or an organization? What are the author's qualifications? Is the site affiliated with the government, an educational institution, a private foundation, or a company?

2. Scope. What is the intended audience of the site? What body of information is covered? How does the scope relate to the author's expertise?

3. Timeliness. When was the information posted? How often is the site updated?

4. Presentation. Are there misspellings or grammatical errors? Are there broken links?

5. Mission. Does the site have an obvious agenda? Is there any obvious bias?

6. Review. Has information on the site been peer reviewed? Is there a mechanism for comments, feedback, or criticism?

Among the most highly reliable websites are those developed by universities and colleges, government health and science agencies, professional scientific societies, and private research foundations. However, even websites hosted by reputable organizations should be critically evaluated. In fact, it is best to make a habit of assessing the reliability of *every* secondary source; with minor modification, the previous guidelines can be used for printed sources.

OBSERVATIONS, EXPLANATIONS, EXPERIMENTS

Scientific studies are rooted in previous work, yet seek to expand the boundaries of existing knowledge. A key aspect of the Introduction is describing the study's purpose within the context of prior studies. Appreciating this function of the Introduction requires an understanding of the different sorts of activities that make up scientific methodology. Scientists make observations, propose explanations, and test explanations. Although these processes are interconnected, studies do not necessarily address all three of them. In reading the Introduction, you should identify the main purpose of the study and ask questions appropriate to the purpose.

A main goal of biological inquiry is to develop accurate explanations of the natural world. Scientists explore areas where our existing explanations are incomplete. A first step in new research is to collect as many relevant facts as possible. To learn about the observations made by others, scientists read the primary literature and communicate with their colleagues. They also make their own observations, often aided by specialized equipment such as microscopes. Look for evidence of observations in the Introduction. How does previous work form the basis for the current study? What aspects of the research area are incompletely understood? What new observations led the scientists to undertake the work?

Some studies are mainly observational; for example their purpose might be to sequence a bacterial genome or to survey the species in a region of rainforest. In such cases, ask yourself whether the Introduction justifies the collection of new information. How do the new observations improve upon previous ones? Will the new data set be more complete or detailed? Is some new observational tool or technique available? Will the new data lead to new explanations or revision of current ones?

In some instances, specific research questions arise from observations. Suppose you observe that a bird is capable of unusually fast flight. What questions arise from this observation? One type of question asks *how* the bird achieves rapid flight. What anatomical, physiological, and biochemical properties contribute to its speed? Another type of question asks *why* the bird flies fast. Is the function to avoid predators, attack prey, migrate quickly, or some combination? New questions also arise when observations contradict expectations. Scientists recently found blood vessels in a *Tyrannosaurus rex* skeleton, countering the conventional wisdom that dinosaur soft tissue is not preserved and leading to a whole new set of questions about dinosaur evolution, anatomy, and physiology.

Choosing which questions to pursue is a crucial decision for scientists. Scientists may share a new research idea with other members of their research group. They will assess the scientific merits of the project. How important will the results be? Will a key research problem be resolved? They will consider how likely it is to succeed. Are there major technical hurdles to be overcome? Does the group have the time and money to pursue the project? Will it be possible to get funding? Finally, they will evaluate practical issues. Is another research group pursuing a similar project? Would the project help a student move towards completion of a degree? Will someone need to spend weekends taking care of animals or cell lines? In the end, both scientific and practical factors influence whether a project is pursued.

When scientists decide to tackle a research question, they carefully gather relevant observations and then propose an explanation. Scientific explanations take the form of **theories** and **hypotheses**. All scientific explanations are subject to revision, but theories are generally well-established explanations, while hypotheses are usually tentative explanations that have not been fully tested. Also, theories have broader implications than hypotheses, which tend to have a narrower focus.

The chief purpose of some papers is to synthesize observations and evidence into a new theory. If so, consider whether the authors justify the need for it. What biological area does the theory address? Are there existing theories that cover the same area? What are the inadequacies of existing theories? Also examine the strategy for developing a new theory. Why is this paper's approach better than that of previous workers? What experimental data or observations form the basis for the theory? What strategy or logic will be used to develop it? Will a mathematical model be constructed? Is there a plan to test the accuracy of the theory against the available evidence?

Single studies rarely attempt to test entire theories; more commonly studies test specific hypotheses. Hypotheses are tentative explanations. They are based on evidence accumulated through experiments and observations, and they are influenced by the prevailing theories. Good hypotheses lead to specific predictions that can either be contradicted or supported by experiments. When scientists repeatedly obtain experimental results inconsistent with the predictions of a hypothesis, then it must be discarded or substantially revised. When experimental results are consistent with predictions of a hypothesis, it gains support and can be tested further. Those that withstand rigorous and repeated testing become well accepted.

Hypotheses are often stated towards the end of the Introduction. They may be stated explicitly: "We hypothesized that drug X lowers blood pressure by dilating blood vessels." Sometimes they are stated without using the term hypothesis: "We tested whether drug X lowers blood pressure by dilating blood vessels." Or they might be stated as competing possibilities: "One possibility is that drug X lowers blood pressure by dilating blood vessels. However, it is also possible that it lowers blood pressure by causing increased urinary output."

Carefully consider the hypothesis. The Introduction should relate it to previous research. Have the authors made a convincing case for the importance of testing the hypothesis? Does it follow logically from prior research results? Also assess the relationship between the hypothesis and the theory. Is the hypothesis so central to the theory that its rejection would be a challenge to the theory itself? Or does the hypothesis deal with a peripheral aspect of the main theory? If the Introduction contains an outline of how the authors plan to test predictions of the hypothesis, think about the relationship between the experimental strategy and the hypothesis. Does the strategy constitute a rigorous test of the hypothesis? Is it possible to imagine a finding that would contradict predictions of the hypothesis?

SCIENCE AS A CYCLICAL PROCESS

Observation, explanation, and experiments form an interconnected cycle (Figure 2). Observations and experimental results make up the accumulated evidence that is synthesized into explanations, including theories and hypotheses. These explanations are tested by experiments and also motivate new observations. So the accumulated evidence guides the theories and hypotheses that scientists propose. In turn, theories and hypotheses guide the experiments scientists perform and the observations they make. As this cycle proceeds, evidence accumulates and theories become increasingly refined.

Reasoning in science is sometimes from general to specific and sometimes from specific to general. Development of theories moves from specific observations and results to general explanations with far-reaching implications. In contrast, testing of theories moves from the general to the specific as the reasoning proceeds from broad theoretical frameworks to more specific hypotheses and finally to even more specific predictions about experimental results.

You will occasionally read a paper that does not fit neatly into the framework we've discussed. Scientists draw on diverse tactics, and they may apply more than one strategy in a study. So, use this section as a guide towards understanding the Introduction, but don't be surprised to find creative approaches that defy this simple framework. And remember that consensus in science comes from the accumulated findings of many studies, so it is always wise to assess how each study relates to other research.

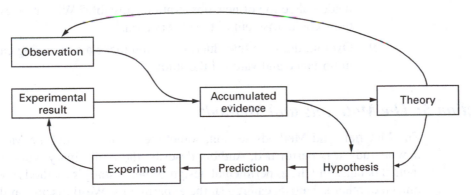

FIGURE 2. A simple model of scientific methodology.

SECTION 4 EXERCISES

Using a research article as an example, complete the following exercises:

1. Read the Introduction section of the paper. What is its main research area?

2. List the 10 most important terms used in the Introduction and give a definition for each term.

3. Identify two or three key previous studies that are described in the Introduction. Describe this previous work in your own words.

4. Are there areas of controversy in the research area? If so, what are they?

5. What new research question does the paper address? Why is this research question important? How does it extend previous work?

6. Does the paper test a hypothesis? If not, go to question 7. If so, restate in your own words the study's hypothesis. How does the hypothesis relate to the main theory? If the hypothesis is rejected, will the main theory be challenged? What predictions of the hypothesis are tested in the study? Describe a finding that would contradict the hypothesis and one that would support it.

7. Does the paper aim to develop a new theory or refine an existing one? If not, go to question 8. If so, is there an existing theory that addresses the research question? What are the shortcomings of the existing theory? What information, experimental or observational, is available to guide development of a new or refined theory? What approach does the paper take towards the refinement or development of theory?

8. Does the paper aim to collect a new set of observations? If not, go to question 9. If so, describe the new set of observations. How will they extend previous observations? Has a new technique or technology made collection of new observations possible? What new explanations could arise out of the observations?

9. Overall, does the Introduction section make a convincing case for the importance and value of the study?

Section 5: The Materials and Methods

The Materials and Methods section, sometimes simply called the Methods, tells how a study was performed. Authors describe the preliminary work, the experimental details, and the experimental design. When a study's methods are well documented, other scientists can repeat the experiments. We'll discuss in this section how to assess the effectiveness of a study's methods.

PRELIMINARY WORK AND APPROVALS

Scientists often conduct preliminary studies before they do the work reported in a paper. They may need to troubleshoot equipment or develop new methodologies. Preliminary experiments may be needed to optimize procedures. Patience, determination, and problem-solving skills are prerequisites for success during these early stages of a research project. If the authors discuss optimization of techniques or development of new procedures in the Materials and Methods, extensive work may have preceded the reported experiments.

Scientists need permission before starting some studies. If a study involves vertebrate animals or human subjects, scientists must apply to a **review board**. These boards are usually composed of other scientists, ethicists, and members of the general public. Review boards that evaluate human studies assess the balance between benefits and risks. In assessing benefits, the board considers whether the study will produce important findings. Are there general societal benefits? Will the subjects directly benefit, such as in a study that tests a disease treatment? Is the experiment well designed? Has the work already been done? In assessing risks, the board considers the chance of physical or psychological harm to the subjects. Will the researchers undertake every reasonable measure to minimize harm? Will subjects be completely informed of the study's procedures and risks and then asked to give their **informed consent**? Will subjects be unfairly coerced into participating, for example through unreasonable financial incentives or by the implication that participation is a condition of employment?

The review boards that assess animal studies are usually distinct from those that assess human studies. However, they consider many of the same factors. Animal review boards also ask whether the scientists have considered alternate models that would reduce the number of animals used. For example, could tissue culture replace some of the animal studies? If a study was approved by a review board, this is usually stated in the paper, often in the first few paragraphs of the Materials and Methods. Look for evidence of such review, especially if you have questions about the treatment of animals or human subjects. Other aspects of a study may also require approval, for example use of controlled drugs or radioactive materials. Again, look for evidence of such approvals in the Materials and Methods.

NUTS AND BOLTS: EXPERIMENTAL DETAILS

The Materials and Methods is often packed with technical terminology and methodological detail, sometimes making it difficult to read. How can you handle this dense information? One strategy is to evaluate the variables that were assessed, measured, manipulated, or controlled. In most studies, you will find three separate types of variables: dependent variables, independent variables, and controlled variables.

Dependent Variables

Dependent variables change in response to other variables. The purpose of many experiments is to characterize dependent variables and how they change under different conditions. For example, in a study of volume regulation in fish cells, cell volume is the dependent variable. Experiments might examine how it changes in response to other variables, such as the osmolarity of the surrounding fluid. Take care to identify the dependent variables, because these are often the study's focus.

Measurement of dependent variables may require sophisticated techniques. Be sure that you understand the key techniques used in a paper. You can't evaluate the results if you don't know how they were obtained. Some techniques involve a number of steps. Suppose for example a study examines changes in gene expression during cell volume regulation. A first step would be to isolate RNA, a process which includes several centrifugation and incubation steps. Relying only on the text of the Materials and Methods, you might find it difficult to see how each part of a multi-step procedure fits together. To better understand a technique, try to draw a flowchart that outlines its steps. Figure 3 shows how such a flowchart might look for a standard RNA isolation procedure. When you depict a technique this way, the methodological details as well as the overall strategy become apparent. Basic procedures may not be described in the Materials and Methods because the authors assume the audience is familiar with them. In such cases, you may need to consult secondary sources to learn more.

Independent Variables

Independent variables potentially influence the dependent variable. In some cases they are directly manipulated by the experimenter. Other times they are measured but not manipulated. Let's consider again a study of cell volume regulation. Osmolarity of the fluid outside cells is an independent variable because it is predicted to affect cell volume. Osmolarity can be manipulated, for example, by placing cells into solutions of different solute concentration. Suppose, however, we were interested in whether or not cell volume regulation is different in the cells of marine versus freshwater fish. In this case, the independent variable is the habitat of the fish. Although we may be unable to change this variable, we could still examine its effect by studying fish collected from different habitats. Some studies test multiple independent variables; be sure to identify all of them.

Controlled Variables

A difficulty in many studies is that numerous factors other than those under investigation could affect the outcome. For this reason, scientists seeking to measure the influence of independent variables strive to control other variables; these are called **controlled variables**. For example, studying the effect of osmolarity on cell volume requires that other factors, such as temperature and pH, are held constant. Variables can sometimes be controlled through experimental design. Imagine that

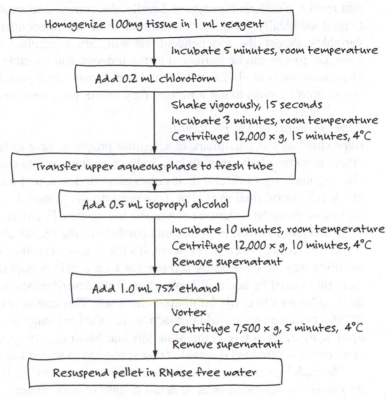

FIGURE 3. Flowchart of a standard RNA isolation procedure, modified from instructions for Trizol reagent, Invitrogen.

a difference was detected between cell volume regulation of a marine compared to a freshwater fish. Can this difference be attributed to the different habitat or is it due to some other difference between the two species? Studying a single species, such as salmon, that migrates between marine and freshwater environments would make species a controlled variable. Scientists seek to control as many variables as they can, because doing so enables them to draw stronger conclusions. Look closely at the Materials and Methods to see which variables the investigators have controlled. Consider whether there are other variables that could have influenced the results but were not controlled.

Controls

Many experimental designs use **control groups**. Don't confuse these with controlled variables; they're not exactly the same. Control groups usually receive a treatment where the independent variable is unchanged from the normal or ordinary value. They can therefore serve as a comparison for the **experimental groups** that receive a different treatment. Ideally, the control and experimental groups are treated identically except for the difference in the independent variable. If so, all variables except the independent variable are controlled and any difference between groups can be attributed to the independent variable. Unfortunately, this ideal situation is rarely found in actual experiments, and you should carefully consider control groups to see how well they mirror the experimental groups.

Reproducibility and Repeatability

Reproducibility is a hallmark of scientific progress. Scientists repeat the work of others because verifying a study's findings strengthens its conclusions. Scientists also regularly try to extend their colleagues' findings, and a first step is to repeat and verify the original work. For these reasons, the Materials and Methods must be written so that other scientists can repeat the studies. Extensive detail is required to meet this requirement. Experimental conditions and technical detail must be thoroughly described, because even small differences may alter outcomes. Standard methods may be covered by a reference to a previous paper, but any deviations from them must be noted. When authors fully describe their methods, they enable their colleagues to easily build upon the work. This can save other scientists huge efforts, because successful approaches are often the outcome of time-consuming optimization. As you read the Materials and Methods, ask yourself whether sufficient detail is provided to enable other scientists to repeat the study.

Methodological detail may be useful if you're working in a research lab, but do you really need that level of detail simply to understand a paper? Perhaps not. But you will still sometimes need to consider procedural details. Consider two papers that come to contradictory conclusions. Examining how each study was performed might uncover differences that explain the discrepancies. You may also need to refer to the Materials and Methods as you assess the Results. Suppose a paper reports that "women who ate a high-carbohydrate diet ran 15% longer than those who ate a normal diet." You would want to know many methodological details before interpreting this result. How many women were tested? What were their ages? Were they trained athletes? How were they selected to participate in the study? What was the composition of the diet? How fast did the women run? The Materials and Methods section should supply these details. One way to use the Materials and Methods is to consult it for details that are necessary to interpret the Results.

THE BIG PICTURE: EXPERIMENTAL DESIGN

Convincing findings arise when a study's design is well matched to its purpose. As we'll see below, different purposes call for different experimental approaches. In reading the Materials and Methods, one of your main tasks is to assess the experimental design's effectiveness. Correlative studies are most appropriate for describing the **patterns** in nature. Causative studies are most effective at establishing the **causal factors** that explain those patterns.

Correlative Studies: Patterns and Connections

In **correlative studies**, scientists do not manipulate independent variables, but instead exploit preexisting variation in them. For this reason, they are often called **retrospective studies**. They are also sometimes referred to as **cross-sectional studies** or **observational studies**. Because correlative studies can investigate multiple independent variables simultaneously without artificial manipulation of the conditions, they are an excellent means for identifying connections between variables.

Let's look at an example. Suppose that scientists suspect that an insecticide, used on vegetables, causes cancer in humans. A correlative approach would be to identify people who have been exposed to the insecticide and compare their cancer rates to a control group. Cancer rate is the dependent variable in this study, while insecticide exposure is the independent variable. If cancer rates are the same in both populations, then the insecticide probably does not cause cancer. If cancer rates are higher in the exposed population, a correlation has been established between cancer rate and insecticide exposure.

Correlative Studies: Challenges and Limitations

A challenge in correlative studies is that many independent variables may be correlated with the dependent variable. For example, family history, diet, exercise, and smoking all might affect cancer rates. Interpretation is complicated if multiple factors are different between the control and experimental groups. Thus, scientists attempt to match the groups, so that variables other than those being studied are the same. If scientists can't match the groups, they measure variables known to influence the dependent variable and use statistical techniques to account for the differences. In assessing a correlative study, consider whether the investigators have accounted for all the variables that could influence the outcome.

Correlative studies cannot demonstrate causation; they can only suggest it. One issue is that cause and effect can be confused. Consider a study that demonstrates a correlation between exercise and healthy heart function. One possibility is that exercise causes improvements in heart function. But it is also possible that people with healthy hearts are more likely to exercise; in this case, a healthy heart contributes to high levels of physical activity rather than the reverse. Another issue is that independent variables may be correlated with changes in a dependent variable even if they're not causative. In the insecticide example, consider the possibility that other cancer risk factors are present in the part of the country where the insecticide was used. If so, the insecticide could be associated with cancer risk only because it is correlated with a causative factor, not because it is a cause itself. Correlative and causative studies are often used together. Correlative studies can point out possible causes, which can then be investigated in causative studies.

Causative Studies: Between-Groups Design

In **causative studies,** scientists manipulate an independent variable and measure the effect on a dependent variable. In a **between-groups design**, experimental groups receive a treatment while a *separate* control group does not. For example, in Figure 4A, the experimental group exercises and the control group does not. The effect of the experimental treatment can be determined by comparing post-treatment measurements in the control and experimental groups. Random assignment of subjects into groups minimizes the chance that they differ in factors other than the manipulated independent variable. Measurements on experimental and control groups can be made at the same time under identical conditions, ensuring that variables other than those under study are held constant. However, because separate individuals are assigned to control and experimental groups, between groups designs do not control for interindividual variability. When such variability is high, the groups are more likely to differ from each other prior to the treatment, and it can be difficult to differentiate between preexisting differences and those due to the treatment.

Causative Studies: Repeated-Measures Design

Repeated-measures designs control for differences among individuals by studying the *same* subjects after exposure to different treatments. A simple repeated measures design is to make measurements **before and after** a treatment (Figure 4B). The treatment effect can then be expressed as the *difference* between the before and after measurements in the same individual, controlling for interindividual variability. This makes it easier to detect differences, allowing smaller sample sizes to be used. Note that in the before-and-after design, time-related variables are not controlled since the treatment effect is always measured after the control. This can be a problem when the variables are influenced by the time of day or when making an initial measurement affects later measurements.

A **cross-over** repeated-measures design addresses these issues. Cross-over designs are similar to between-groups designs, except that the same individuals undergo both the control and experimental treatments on separate occasions. Treatments can be matched so that only the studied variables differ. To control for effects due to the order of treatment, subjects can be randomly assigned to receive the experimental or control treatment first. Figure 4A would depict a cross-over design if the same subjects performed the control and exercise treatments on separate days.

Model Systems

Causative studies often employ **model systems.** Models are alternative experimental systems that save time and money and allow experiments that would otherwise be impossible. A laboratory animal might be used instead of humans, or tissue culture might be used in place of a living animal. However, care must be taken in extrapolating from the model. Scientists choose model systems with great care, balancing their

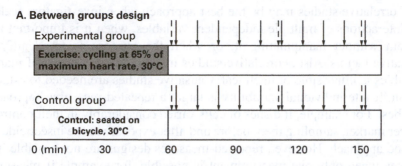

A. Between groups design

Experimental group

| Exercise: cycling at 65% of maximum heart rate, 30°C |

Control group

| Control: seated on bicycle, 30°C |

0 (min)   30   60   90   120   150

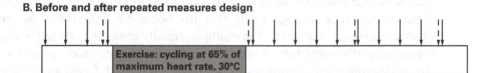

B. Before and after repeated measures design

| | Exercise: cycling at 65% of maximum heart rate, 30°C | |

0 (min)   30   60   90   120   150   180

FIGURE 4. Timelines of two different experimental designs. Solid arrows represent blood pressure measurements; dotted arrows represent blood samples. Panel A shows a between-groups design if separate subjects form the control and experimental groups. The same timelines would depict a cross-over repeated-measures design if the same subjects received control and experimental treatments on different occasions. Panel B shows a before-and-after design.

advantages and disadvantages. If a study uses a model system, you should consider whether it makes the experiments easier to perform and also assess how well it represents the system it replaces.

Let's return to the example of insecticide and cancer risk. Conducting a causative study of insecticide use and cancer risk in humans may be impossible; exposing humans to a suspected carcinogen is clearly unethical. Instead, suppose that carcinogenicity could be assessed by applying the insecticide to cultured cells and assessing their production of a cancer marker. In this case, you would want to assess whether findings in these tissue culture experiments are applicable to insecticide exposure in humans. For example, is it possible that the insecticide is broken down when ingested by a human but is not when applied to cultured cells?

Evaluating Experimental Design

The Materials and Methods may not explicitly state what type of study was conducted or which groups are the controls. Sometimes, you can make sense out of the experimental design by diagramming it. Draw a timeline for each experimental group and indicate treatments and measurements on it (Figure 4). The study design and control groups should become obvious. Combine this with technique flowcharts (Figure 3), and you'll have a complete visual representation of the study.

Correlative studies may be the best approach when investigators seek to study the interactions of multiple independent variables, when it is important to study a system without manipulating it, or when the purpose is to identify possible causative factors. Also, correlative studies may be the only option if manipulating variables is impossible or unethical. Causative studies are needed to establish causation. If interindividual variability is large, a repeated-measures approach is usually best. For example, if dishes of cells varied considerably in their control level of cancer marker, sampling them before and after exposure to the insecticide would be a good approach. However, repeated-measures designs are not possible in circumstances when only one measurement is possible, for example if measurement of cancer marker damaged the cells. Repeated-measures designs also don't work well if the subjects are changing rapidly over time because it is then possible that they've changed between treatments. For example, rapidly growing cells might display different properties over time, making comparisons on separate occasions difficult. Try to determine why a particular study design was used. Consider the study's purpose as well as the limitations and constraints of the experimental system.

Critically consider the controls in causative studies. What would be an appropriate control treatment in the experiment of insecticide exposure in tissue culture cells? To decide we must know how the experimental treatment was performed. Exposing cells to insecticide might include preparing a solution of insecticide in solvent, pipetting the insecticide solution onto the cells, and then mixing by gentle shaking. A good control would match everything except the insecticide exposure, for example by pipetting a solution containing the same solvent without insecticide onto the cells. Check to see whether there are differences between the experimental and control groups other than the studied variables.

SECTION 5 EXERCISES

Using a research article as an example, complete the following exercises:

1. Was preliminary work done before the reported experiments were performed? How does the preliminary work relate to the reported experiments?

2. Did the authors obtain approvals from animal or human review boards or other regulatory agencies? Do you have questions or concerns about treatment of human or animal subjects?

3. List the variables studied. Differentiate between independent, dependent, and controlled variables.

4. How do the authors measure the dependent variables? Were the independent variables manipulated by the investigators? How were other variables controlled? Did the investigators fail to control any important variables?

5. Choose a key technique and draw a flowchart to depict it.

6. Do the Materials and Methods provide enough detail for another scientist to repeat the work?

7. Draw a timeline depicting the experimental design. Indicate the timing of measurements and treatments.

8. Was a model system used in the study? If so, what experimental advantages does it have over the system it replaces? How well does it mimic the system it replaces?

9. Describe the overall study design. Classify it as correlative or causative. If it is causative, is it a repeated measures or a between-groups design? Does the design fit well with the study's main purpose?

Section 6: The Results

The Results, together with the Materials and Methods, are the core of a study. New observations, data, and findings are presented in the Results. In this section, we discuss strategies to help you assess the primary data.

Scientists collect data in many forms, including numerical output from instruments and visual information such as photographs and micrographs. Unprocessed data must be recorded in a timely, accurate, and lasting form. Human memory is not always trustworthy, and thus the most reliable records are made immediately. Scientists keep a lab or field **notebook** where they record their methods and data. You can view the Results section as a translation of unprocessed data from the notebook into a succinct and easily understood form. Rarely does this mean sharing all the data in exactly the form they were collected. Data are analyzed, sorted, and synthesized before they are presented. The notebook is also important as physical proof that the work was actually performed. In the rare case of an accusation of research fraud, it becomes an important piece of evidence.

DEALING WITH VARIABILITY: STATISTICS

In this section, we discuss basic statistical principles needed to assess biological studies. When reading articles, you may need to consult a statistical manual for more information about specific statistical tests (see Resources, p. 43).

Variability is ubiquitous in measurements of biological systems. **Technical variability**, or **measurement error**, arises any time a measurement is made. No technique is perfect, and variability is introduced when measurements deviate unpredictably from actual values. Scientists always seek to minimize technical variability because it complicates data interpretation, but it can never be completely eliminated. **Biological variability** refers to real differences between individuals. Because biological variability represents actual differences, there's no way to completely eliminate it. In fact, scientists sometimes want to study it because it plays a key role in processes such as natural selection. Although biological variability can't be eliminated, careful experimental design can minimize its influence. For example, when studying animals, matching factors such as age, weight, and sex can reduce biological variability.

Due to variability, biologists need to make multiple measurements to fully characterize a system. These measurements constitute a **data set**. Sometimes an entire data set is shown in a paper. If the heart rate of six cyclists has been measured, they might all be presented in a table. More commonly, data sets are summarized. Sometimes, data sets are presented graphically, as **histograms** or **frequency distributions**. Some distributions are **symmetrical** (Figure 5A). **Normal distributions** are a specific type of symmetrical distribution that form a characteristic bell-shaped curve. Many statistical tests assume a normal distribution, a condition not always met in biological data sets. Nonsymmetrical distributions can have various shapes. For example, they may be skewed in one direction (Figure 5B). Distributions may also be **unimodal**, having a single peak (Figures 5A and 5B), or **multimodal**, having more than one peak. In evaluating data, try to get a sense of the way the values are distributed. Unfortunately, this can be difficult to assess in many papers, because the needed data are often not provided.

Descriptive Statistics: Central Tendency and Variability
Data sets can also be summarized by describing two features: **central tendency** and **variability**. Central tendency describes the typical or representative value. **Means**, the arithmetic average of the points in a data set, are the most common way of representing central tendency. They work particularly well with symmetrical data sets. **Medians** are the middle value when the points are arranged from highest to lowest; **modes** are the most common value in a data set. Medians and modes can be useful with nonsymmetrical data sets, such as those that are skewed in one direction. In these data sets, the most extreme outlying values can have a disproportionate effect on the mean, pulling it away from the central tendency. Most papers in biology summarize data using means. Be aware that means are only a partial representation of a data set. The shape of the distribution and the amount of variability are also important.

Two common measures of variability are the **range**, the minimum and maximum values, and the **standard deviation,** which represents an adjusted average distance between individual data points and the mean. A large standard deviation indicates high variability, meaning the data are more spread out compared to a data set with a small standard deviation. For a normal distribution, about 68% of the values are within one standard deviation of the mean, while about 95% of the values are within two standard deviations. Values are often reported as a measure of the central tendency ± a measure of variability; for instance mean ± standard deviation. In assessing results, consider the magnitude of the variability in the context

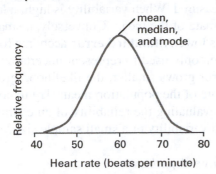

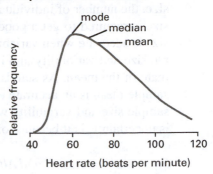

FIGURE 5. Frequency distributions. Relative frequency is the proportion of all the values in a data set that fall into a particular range. Panel A shows a symmetrical distribution. Panel B shows an asymmetrical distribution with a positive skew.

of the central tendency. For example, a standard deviation of 1 second may be irrelevant when comparing a mean difference of several hours, but crucial when evaluating a mean difference of a few seconds.

Inferential Statistics: From a Sample to a Population
It's often desirable to generalize from a studied group, the **sample**, to a broader group, the **population**. For example, scientists are probably not just interested in how *one particular* flask of *Escherichia coli* responds to altered glucose concentration; more likely they hope their findings will apply to other cultures of *E. coli* as well. **Inferential statistics** enable scientists to generalize from a specific sample to a wider population. Uncertainty always exists in this process, and inferential statistical approaches therefore lead to statements of *probabilities* rather than certainties.

If you want to know the mean heart rate of women at your college, one approach would be to study every woman on campus. If this was impractical, an alternate approach would be to study a properly selected sample and then generalize to the broader population. If heart rate was measured in 10 women, the mean of this sample would be an estimate of the population's mean. Repeating the measurement with ten different women would probably return a slightly different mean. The results in most papers reflect a similar scenario; some individuals are sampled as representatives of a larger population. A crucial step in assessing such results is determining how accurately the sample reflects the population. First determine what population the scientists are interested in, and then assess how well the sample represents this population. For example, a sample of varsity athletes would probably not be representative of the heart rates of the general campus population, while a random sample of enrolled students would be more representative.

The reliability of an estimate is also affected by the variability and the **sample size**, the number of individuals measured. When variability is high, a large sample size is required to get a good estimate of the mean. Conversely, a smaller sample size is adequate when variability is lower. **Standard error** accounts for both sample size and variability and is commonly used to represent uncertainty in an estimate of the mean. As standard error grows smaller, the likelihood grows that the sample mean is an accurate estimate of the population mean. Try to consider both sample size and variability when evaluating the reliability of an estimate. If there is uncertainty, is it because of high variability or a small sample size?

Statistical Tests: Null and Alternative Hypotheses
Suppose you sampled 20 men and 20 women on your campus and found a difference in heart rates between sexes. One possibility is that a real difference exists between men and women on campus. Another is that the measured difference occurred by chance as a result of sampling only part of variable populations; for example, the sample of women might have inadvertently included several women with higher than average heart rates. Inferential statistics can help distinguish between these possibilities by determining the *probability* that a difference in sample means is due to a true difference in the population.

Many statistical tests differentiate between a **null hypothesis** and an **alternative hypothesis**. These hypotheses are constructed so that only one can be true. For example, if the null hypothesis states there is no difference between treatments, the alternative hypothesis states that there is a difference. The alternative hypothesis is the one that requires strong support in order to be accepted. To establish a rigorous test of the alternative hypothesis, statistical tests begin with the assumption that the null hypothesis is true. The alternative hypothesis gains support only when the null hypothesis is rejected. The bottom line is that the alternative hypothesis is rigorously tested while the null hypothesis is not.

Statistical hypotheses are only valid when they are developed before data are collected or examined. It's always possible to develop a hypothesis that fits a particular data set after it is collected, but when this is done the hypothesis has not been rigorously tested. Assessing whether a hypothesis was developed before or after conducting the experiments can be difficult. One clue is whether it was mentioned in an earlier paper.

The alternative hypothesis usually states the interesting result: that there is an effect, difference, or correlation. Consequently, the null hypothesis usually states that there is no effect, no difference, or no correlation. Since the alternative hypothesis is rigorously tested, an interesting result is only accepted when there is strong support for it. Suppose we are interested in determining whether there is a difference between the heart rates of men and women. The null hypothesis would be that there is no difference, and the alternative hypothesis would be that there is a difference. If the null hypothesis is rejected, a difference between men and women would be strongly supported. Papers often state only the alternative hypothesis, but you need to understand both the null and alternative hypotheses to assess statistical tests. If the statistical hypotheses are not explicitly stated, try to determine them yourself.

Positive Results

Rejection of the null hypothesis is a **positive result**, because the alternative hypothesis is strongly supported. However, statistical tests do not reject null hypotheses with absolute certainty. There always remains the possibility that a null hypothesis has been mistakenly rejected. Rejecting a true null hypothesis is a **Type I error**, also called a **false-positive error**. Biologists are willing to accept only a low possibility of making such errors, because they can lead to the erroneous acceptance of the interesting result described by the alternative hypothesis.

Inferential statistics assess the probability that a false-positive error will be committed. Many statistical tests return a number called a **p-value**. Findings are labeled as **statistically significant** when the p-value is less than a preestablished **significance level**. A typical significance level in biology studies is 0.05; this means that the null hypothesis will be rejected if there is less than a 5% chance of doing so mistakenly. When considering statistically significant results, always assess the probability that an error has been made. If p-values are reported, they directly indicate the likelihood of making a false-positive error. Very low p-values indicate that the null hypothesis can be rejected with high certainty. In other words, as p-values decrease, the chance of making a false-positive error also decreases.

Also consider the significance levels used in a study. A low significance level ensures a small chance of committing a false-positive error. For example, a low significance level might be warranted when testing a risky drug treatment in an experimental animal, because a very high likelihood of effectiveness might be needed prior to human testing. On the other hand, less certainty might be acceptable in preliminary studies with high variability or lower sample sizes.

Because each study has some probability of making a false-positive error, such errors inevitably slip into the published literature. Thus, some of the statistically significant findings reported in papers are false-positive results. Reproducing findings is an antidote to this problem. Statistical significance is unlikely to arise erroneously in several experiments, especially if they are done with different conditions or methodologies.

Negative Results

Negative results arise when the null hypothesis is not rejected; in such cases the alternative hypothesis is not supported. As with positive results, it is always possible that a negative result is mistaken. Failing to reject a false null hypothesis leads to a **Type II error**, also called a **false-negative error**. In this case, an alternative hypothesis that should have been accepted is not. In contrast to a false-positive error, the probability that a false-negative error has occurred usually cannot be determined. Therefore, when the null hypothesis is not rejected, it is not appropriate to accept it or to reject the alternative hypothesis. In fact, the evidence may even favor the alternative hypothesis. For example, in the case of a p-value of 0.06 in a study where the threshold is set at 0.05, the null hypothesis would not be rejected. Also, a failure to reject the null hypothesis might occur because the experimental design was flawed or the sample size was too small. Consider the possibility of false-negative results when differences are found to be not statistically significant.

Negative results can be hard to publish. Convincingly demonstrating no difference between treatments or no connection between variables is difficult. Also, findings of no effect generally don't generate the same excitement as positive results. But there are good reasons to publish well-designed studies that produce negative results. One reason is that it saves other scientists from repeating the same study; another is that finding no effect might have important biological implications. Ruling out one cause might strengthen the case for another.

Biological Relevance
A finding of statistical significance does not necessarily imply that a result is biologically meaningful. Suppose that two species have a statistically significant difference in mean body temperature: 37.1°C for one species and 37.2°C for the other. Does a 0.1°C difference in body temperature have any important biological implications? Conversely, further study of a biologically interesting difference, such as a 3°C difference in body temperature between species, might be worthwhile even without proof of statistical significance. Remember that false-negative results are possible. Statistical significance might arise with experimental refinements or increased sample sizes. As you assess the results, look carefully at the magnitude of differences. Are there large differences that fail to reach statistical significance? Do statistically significant differences vary enough for there to be biological consequences?

VISUALIZING RESULTS: TABLES AND GRAPHS

Results can be presented as pictures, graphs, tables, or as statements in the text. Consider how data are presented; this gives you a sense of which results the authors wish to emphasize. Tables can concisely present large data sets, but it's tough to emphasize particular findings using a table. Presenting data in graphs takes a bit more space than in tables, but graphs are more effective in illustrating differences. The most important findings are ordinarily presented in graphs and tables, because these attract the most attention from readers. Key findings are also emphasized in the Results text. We'll focus below on graphs; you can apply a similar approach to reading tables.

Graphs
Take your time assessing graphs, because they consolidate large amounts of information. A graph's purpose can be discerned by determining the dependent and independent variables and reading the **figure legend**. Independent variables are ordinarily shown on the **x-axis**, and dependent variables are plotted on the **y-axis**.

Imagine that investigators have identified a new species of bacteria from a hot spring and have tested its growth rate at two different temperatures (Figure 6). In this graph, specific growth rate is the dependent variable, temperature is the independent variable, and comparison of growth rates at two temperatures is the purpose. Consider how the purpose of the experiment plotted on a graph relates to the study's overall purpose. For example, why is the comparison of growth rates shown in Figure 6 important? You may need to return to the Introduction for a reminder of the study's goals.

Examine the graph's **units** and **axis scale**. First, determine the unit of measurement, which is often given in parentheses after the **axis label**. Notice that specific growth rate in Figure 6 is expressed as h^{-1}. What does this unit mean? How was growth rate measured? What experimental conditions were used? You will find answers to some questions in the figure legend, but you may also need to check the Materials and Methods. Also assess what range of values was measured by looking at the y-axis scale. In Figure 6, specific growth rates range from about 0.02 h^{-1} to 0.04 h^{-1}. Are these high or low growth rates? You may need to compare values to those from other figures or even other papers in order to get a sense of what the reported numbers mean.

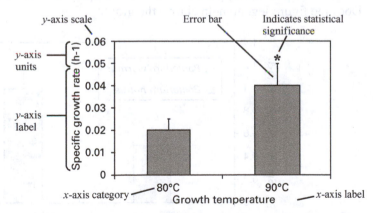

FIGURE 6. Growth rate of the fictional hot springs bacteria *Bacterium warmus* measured at 80°C and 90°C. Bars represent means ± standard error. $n = 12$ for each species. Significant differences between treatments ($p < 0.05$, Student's *t*-test) are indicated by a (*).

Once you understand the purpose and methods behind a graph, try to discern the major patterns in the data. What are the major trends? Are the differences between treatments large or small? Consider measures of variability, which are often given as **error bars** projecting above and/or below data points. How variable are the data? Is the variability consistent across treatments? Do any data points fail to follow the overall trend? Read the figure legend closely; it often gives important information such as the sample size (often abbreviated as n), the type of variability shown in the error bars, and how the data were statistically evaluated. In Figure 6, the sample size was 12, the error bars depict standard error, statistical differences were evaluated with a Student's t-test, and the significance level was set at 0.05. Sometimes statistically significant findings are indicated by marks on the graph. Read the figure legend to learn how these marks are used. In Figure 6, the * symbol above the 90°C bar is used to show that the difference in growth rates at the two temperatures is statistically significant.

Evaluating Data

As you evaluate the results, consider how they've been presented. Let's suppose growth rates of a second hot springs bacterial species were also measured. The graph in Figure 7 emphasizes the difference between the species. The effect of temperature on *Bacterium hottus* is also apparent. But notice that the effect of temperature on *Bacterium warmus*, which was evident in Figure 6, is now difficult to discern in Figure 7 because the y-axis scale has been changed to accommodate the higher growth rates of *Bacterium hottus*. The bottom line is that a graph can emphasize or camouflage different aspects of the data. When reading a graph, ask yourself how the data are presented. Are certain differences highlighted? Are others obscured? Does the presentation reflect the authors' opinions about the data? Do you see interesting patterns that are downplayed in the authors' presentation? Does the figure legend help clarify the graph?

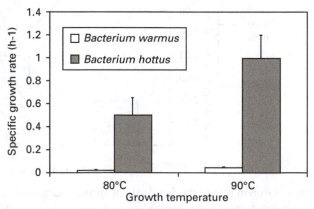

FIGURE 7. Growth rates of two fictional hot springs bacteria measured at 80°C and 90°C. Bars represent means ± standard error. $n = 12$ for each treatment.

Try to evaluate the numerical data without being influenced by how they are presented. One method is to examine the graphs and tables for major trends before reading the Results text. Another strategy is to read the Results section text first, picking out the main statements the authors make about their data. Then, check to see if the numerical data in the tables or graphs support these statements. The key is to develop your understanding of the study's findings and then compare it to what the authors say. If there's a discrepancy, you might have identified a shortcoming in the authors' analysis. On the other hand, you might also have misunderstood the authors, so check your analysis carefully.

Why go through all the trouble to evaluate the primary data yourself? Why not simply read the Results and accept what the authors say? The answer is that only after evaluating the primary data can you critically assess the study and its conclusions. Just as you can't intelligently review a movie or a book unless you've read it yourself, you can't critically assess a scientific study without personally evaluating its core component: the data.

SECTION 6 EXERCISES

Using a research article as an example, complete the following exercises:

1. How are the data presented in the paper? In pictures, graphs, tables, or text?

2. Choose a key table or graph and use it to answer the following questions. What are the main trends in the data? Are the differences between treatments large or small? How is variability depicted? How variable are the data? How are the data distributed? How is central tendency presented?

3. Summarize each table or graph in the paper in a few sentences. Compare your description to that of the authors.

4. What population is the study interested in examining? Does the study sample only part of the population? Is the sample representative of the entire population?

5. How well do the measurements of the sample estimate the properties of the population? If possible, use standard errors or another statistical measure to support your answer.

6. Choose a key experiment that was analyzed with statistics. State the null and alternative hypotheses. Describe the outcome of the statistical test. If a statistical significance was found, what is the likelihood that a false positive occurred? If no significance was found, can you assess the possibility of a false negative?

7. Are the findings biologically relevant? Are there any findings that didn't reach statistical significance but might be worth further study?

Section 7: The Discussion

The Discussion is an opportunity for authors to explain what their findings mean, to illuminate the key conclusions, and to address potential criticisms. Information is drawn from many different sources, and opinion may mingle with objective fact. Your task is to sort through this information and come to your own conclusions about the study. Be prepared to consult other writings as you read the Discussion. Because it synthesizes information from the rest of the study, you may need to refer back to the Introduction, Materials and Methods, and Results. Since it connects the study to previous work, you may need to consult other research articles.

INTERPRETATION: FINDING MEANING

The Materials and Methods and Results mostly report factual information. While superficial interpretation may be found in the Results, in-depth interpretation is usually confined to the Discussion. **Interpretation** differs from simple reporting of experimental results because it involves describing the *meaning* of the data. Evaluating how well the study fulfills its purpose is a form of interpretation. Authors may describe whether a useful data set was collected, whether the findings support or contradict the hypothesis, or whether a new theory was developed. Another type of interpretation is the synthesis of a study's different findings. Authors may state whether all the study's findings are consistent, whether any results contradict the others, or whether more reliable conclusions can be made when a set of experiments is considered as a whole. Interpretation also includes describing the strengths and weaknesses of a study. Authors may address the shortcomings of their methodologies and the limitations of their conclusions.

Critically reading a paper requires that you completely understand the authors' interpretations, and then compare them to your own. This may seem like a daunting task. Is it even possible to question the interpretations of the authors? Aren't they in a much better position to make interpretations than you? Although you will generally have no basis to question the actual data, you will be able to evaluate *interpretations* of the data. If the authors have presented their methods and results clearly, you have access to all the information that is necessary for developing interpretations. Furthermore, it is possible to arrive at different interpretations than the authors. For example, you may approach the paper from a different perspective, you may have new information that has become available since the authors wrote the article, or you may be more objective in assessing the experimental design and results. A strength of the scientific process is that scientists vigorously challenge each other's interpretations. As you begin developing your own interpretations and assessing those of others, you become an actual participant in the scientific process.

How can you develop your own interpretations? Here's where the hard work you've done assessing the Introduction, Materials and Methods, and Results pays off. Before you read the Discussion, review the other sections with the aim of developing your interpretations. Write these down. Then read the Discussion to see how the authors interpret their findings. You may come across interpretations that didn't occur to you. In these cases, consider whether you agree with the authors, referring if necessary back to the other sections. Developing and assessing interpretations takes practice. You won't be an expert on your first try, but you'll improve with time.

CONNECTIONS: RELATIONSHIP TO OTHER WORK

The Discussion compares the study to previous research, placing the work into the context of a broader research field. This is a key activity, since consensus in science usually emerges from many studies considered together. Authors may discuss how their findings contradict other studies, how previous work supports their conclusions, and how their work extends the knowledge within a field.

Reading the Discussion can be complicated because authors interpret not only their work, but also others' work. Keep track of this as you read by looking for cues that indicate what is being discussed. Previous work is usually identified with a citation: "Physical activity level has been found to be correlated with blood pressure (Smith, *et al.*, 2003)." Or, "Smith and colleagues (2003) found that physical activity level was correlated with blood pressure." Also consider whether a previous study is simply being summarized, as is the case in the examples above, or whether the authors are interpreting or criticizing the study. "Because Smith and colleagues (2003) studied only 10 college-aged males, care must be taken in applying their results to other populations" is an interpretation. Be careful about accepting criticisms of previous work. In fairness to Smith and colleagues, you should check their paper before judging it.

Previous work is often used to support a study's conclusions. The strongest claims can be made when studies by different investigators are consistent. Claims are particularly strengthened when studies using different approaches come to the same conclusion, because it is unlikely that several approaches are flawed. Assess how the study relates to other work. Are the study's conclusions consistent with prior work? Does it use a different approach than previous work? Does the study come to a new conclusion, or is it another piece of evidence supporting a well-studied theory? Does it strengthen a previously shaky conclusion? Authors also describe whether their study conflicts with prior work. Assess such contradictions carefully. Were the previous studies somehow flawed? What differences in methodology may have led to the contradictory results? Why might the new study be more reliable? Here again you may need to consult some of the previous studies to get their perspective.

EXPLANATIONS AND IMPLICATIONS

Scientists have the opportunity to explain their results in the Discussion. For example, when a study demonstrates a cause-and-effect relationship, scientists seek to explain the **mechanism** that connects cause and effect. Suppose a study finds that exercise lowers blood pressure. This conclusion will be strengthened if we have a plausible explanation of how exercise causes a reduction in blood pressure. Sometimes the study itself gives possible clues to the mechanism. Other times mechanisms can be proposed based on previous studies. Look for mechanistic explanations in the Discussion. Do the authors give convincing explanations for their findings? Do their data suggest mechanisms? Are other mechanisms possible?

Some studies are specifically aimed at identifying mechanisms. In such cases you should assess how convincingly the mechanism has been established. Even when a mechanism is clearly demonstrated, a new set of mechanistic questions often arises. As studies accumulate, explanations become more detailed and accurate. The Discussion should give you a sense of this process. How sophisticated are the current mechanistic explanations? Are they well refined or are they general and approximate? Is there more than one competing explanation?

Authors usually describe the significance of their work toward the end of the Discussion. Studies can have scientific significance, practical applications, or both. A study might suggest a new set of research questions, put forward a new theory, or resolve a long-standing controversy. It might support the effectiveness of a new drug, improve a manufacturing process, or aid in the development of a new technology. Examine carefully any claims of significance in the Discussion. Are they justified by the information presented in the paper? Are the implications direct and immediate, or are they tentative and speculative? Sometimes authors describe future work in the Discussion. This can be a clue to the significance of a study. Important work usually leads to exciting new questions to explore.

SECTION 7 EXERCISES

Using a research article as an example, complete the following exercises:

1. How do the authors interpret their findings? Which results do they consider to be most important? Do they claim to support or contradict a hypothesis? Do they synthesize their individual findings into a coherent story?

2. Do the authors address weaknesses of their methods or findings? Do they address possible criticisms?

3. How does your interpretation of the study compare to the authors'?

4. Describe how the study connects to previous research in the field. Is it supported by prior work? Does it contradict any previous conclusions?

5. Do the authors propose an explanation for their findings? Is a plausible mechanism proposed? Is there any evidence to support the proposed mechanism?

6. What are the implications of the study on the research field? Does it suggest new work that needs to be done? What are the next steps that need to be accomplished?

7. What is your overall opinion of the study?

Section 8: Putting it All Together

We've covered lots of specific aspects about reading research articles. Let's think about the themes that have emerged. Here are 10 tips to guide your reading of the primary literature:

1. Focus on methods and results. Try not to be influenced by the way the study is presented, but rather focus your analysis on the experimental design, techniques, and data.

2. Be a skeptic. Ask yourself how strongly the authors' interpretations and conclusions are supported by the evidence.

3. Be fair. Scientific research is difficult, and scientists operate under many constraints. Don't expect studies to be perfect.

4. Read nonlinearly. Exploit the format of research articles to quickly access the information you need. Don't feel compelled to read every line start to finish. Skim the paper to understand its overall approach. Refer to previous sections as necessary.

5. Consider the big picture. Assess where the study fits into the cycle of science, and how it relates to previous research.

6. Consult other sources. Writers of research articles assume their audience has basic knowledge of the area. Consult secondary sources to get the needed background.

7. Take your time. Research articles condense entire studies into a few printed pages. It probably took the authors years to conceive, perform, and publish their work. Be patient and persistent when reading articles.

8. Accept uncertainty. Research articles deal with emerging knowledge and controversial issues. Don't expect to find absolute answers to every question. Each paper is a step in an ongoing process.

9. Expect to be challenged. If you're not an expert in an area, there might be aspects of a paper you can't understand fully. That's OK; you can still learn from those parts of a paper that you can comprehend.

10. Relax and enjoy. Perhaps this is the hardest advice to follow, especially when you're confronted with a complicated paper. But try to approach an article like a puzzle. It's going to take time and effort to make progress, but there's real satisfaction in doing so.

Resources for Students and Educators

WEBSITES

Research articles can be found at the following sites:
    BioMed Central (www.biomedcentral.com).
    Highwire Press (www.highwire.org).
    National Center for Biotechnology Information (www.ncbi.nih.gov).

BOOKS

The following books focus on the scientific method:
    Carey, S. S. (2004). *A beginner's guide to scientific method*. Belmont, CA: Wadsworth/Thomson.
    Gauch Jr., H. G. (2003). *Scientific method in practice*. Cambridge: Cambridge University Press.
    Giere, R. N. (1991). *Understanding scientific reasoning*. Fort Worth: Holt, Rinehart, and Winston.
    Kitcher, P. (1993). *The advancement of science: science without legend, objectivity without illusions*. New York: Oxford University Press.
    Kuhn, T. S. (1970). *The structure of scientific revolutions. International Encyclopedia of Unified Science*, volume 2, number 2. Chicago: University of Chicago Press.
    Popper, K. (1959). *The logic of scientific discovery*. New York: Harper and Row.
    Wilson, E. B. (1952). *An introduction to scientific research*. New York: McGraw-Hill.

The following books focus on reading and writing:
    Adler, M. J. & van Doren, C. (1972). *How to read a book*. New York: Simon and Schuster.
    Allay, M. (1996). *The craft of scientific writing*. New York : Springer.
    Day, R. (1998). *How to write and publish a scientific paper*. Phoenix, AZ: Oryx Press.
    Graff, G., & Birkenstein, C. (2005). *They say/I say: The moves that matter in academic writing*. New York: W. W. Norton.
    McMillan, V. E. (2001). *Writing papers in the biological sciences*. Boston, MA: Bedford Books.
    Pechenik, J. A. (2004). *A short guide to writing about biology*. New York: Pearson/Longman.

The following books focus on experimental design and statistics:

Ambrose, H. W., and K. P. Ambrose. (2002). *Handbook of biological investigation*. Knoxville, TN: Hunter Textbooks.

Barnard, C., Gilbert, F., & McGregor, P. (1993). *Asking questions in biology: design, analysis, and presentation in practical work*. New York: Longman Scientific & Technical.

Gould, J. L. & Gould, G. F. (2002). *Biostats basics: A student handbook*. New York: W.H. Freeman and Company.

Heath, D. (1995). *An introduction to experimental design and statistics for biology*. London: UCL Press.

Quinn, G. P. & Keough, M. J. (2002). *Experimental design and data analysis for biologists*. New York: Cambridge University Press.

Sokal, R. R. (2005). *Biometry*. New York: W.H. Freeman and Company.

Zar, J. H. (2006). *Biostatistical analysis*. Upper Saddle River, NJ: Prentice Hall.

ARTICLES ABOUT READING PAPERS

Gillen, C. M. (2006). Criticism and interpretation: Teaching the persuasive aspects of research articles. *CBE Life Science Education 5*, 34–38.

Levine, E. (2001). Reading your way to scientific literacy. *Journal of College Science Teaching 31*, 122–125.

Muench, S. B. (2000). Choosing primary literature in biology to achieve specific educational goals. *Journal of College Science Teaching, 29*, 255–260.

Mulnix, A. (2003). Investigations of protein structure and function using the scientific literature: An assignment for an undergraduate cell physiology course. *Cell Biology Education, 2*, 248–255.

Pall, M. L. (2000). The value of scientific peer-reviewed literature in a general education science course. *The American Biology Teacher, 62*, 256–258.

Russell, J. S., Martin, L., Curtin, D., Penhale, S. and Trueblood, N. A. (2004). Non-science majors gain valuable insight studying clinical trials literature: an evidence-based medicine library assignment. *Advances in Physiology Education 28*, 188–194.

Smith, G. R. (2001). Guided literature explorations. *Journal of College Science Teaching, 30*, 465–469.

Woodhull-McNeal, A. (1989). Teaching introductory science as inquiry. *College Teaching, 37*, 3–7.

EXAMPLE RESEARCH ARTICLES

Bricelj, V. M., Connell, L., Konoki, K., MacQuarrie, S. P., Scheuer, T., Catterall, W. A., et al. (2005). Sodium channel mutation leading to saxitoxin resistance in clams increases risk of PSP. *Nature, 434:* 763–767.

Carrier D. R., Deban, S. M., & Otterstrom, J., (2002). The face that sank the Essex: Potential function of the spermaceti organ in aggression. *Journal of Experimental Biology, 205*, 1755–1763.

Fleischmann, R. D., Alland, D., Eisen, J. A., Carpenter, L., White, O., Peterson, J., et al. (2002). Whole-genome comparison of *Mycobacterium tuberculosis* clinical and laboratory strains. *Journal of Bacteriology* 184:5479–5490.

Pai, R., Tarnawski, A. S., & Tran, T., (2004). Deoxycholic acid activates β-catenin signaling pathway and increases colon cell cancer growth and invasiveness. *Molecular Biology of the Cell* 15:2156–2163.

Rabbani, M. A., Maruyama, K., Abe, H., Khan, M. A, Katsura, K., Ito, Y., et al. (2003). Monitoring expression profiles of rice genes under cold, drought, and high-salinity stresses and abscisic acid application using cDNA microarray and RNA gel-blot analyses. *Plant Physiology* 133:1755–1767.

Rao, P. K., Kumar, R. M., Farkhondeh, M., Baskerville, S., & Lodish, H. F. (2006). Myogenic factors that regulate expression of muscle-specific microRNAs. *PNAS* 103:8721–8726.

Rocheleau, J. V., Remedi, M. S., Granada, B., Head, W. S., Koster, J. C., Nichols, C. G., et al. (2006). Critical role of gap junction coupled KATP channel activity for regulated insulin secretion. *PLoS Biology* Vol. 4, No. 2, DOI: 10.1371/journal.pbio.0040026.

Schweitzer, M. H., Wittmeyer, J. L., Horner, J. R., & Toporski, J. K. (2005). Soft-tissue vessels and cellular preservation in *Tyrannosaurus rex*. *Science* 25:1952–1955.

Tarnopolsky, M. A., Zawada, C., Richmond, L.B., Carter, S., Shearer, J., Graham, T., et al. (2001). Gender differences in carbohydrate loading are related to energy intake. *Journal of Applied Physiology* 91:225–230.

Weiss, S. L., Lee, E. A., & Diamond, J. (1998). Evolutionary matches of enzyme and transporter capacities to dietary substrate loads in the intestinal brush border. *PNAS* 95:2117–2121.

Wittert, G. A., Turnbull, H., Hope, P., Morley, J. E., & Horowitz, M. (2004). Leptin prevents obesity induced by a high-fat diet after diet-induced weight loss in the marsupial *S. crassicaudata*. *American Journal of Physiology Regulatory Integrative Comparative Physiology* 286:734–739.

Woolley, D. M. & Vernon, G. G. (2001). A study of helical and planar waves on sea urchin sperm flagella, with a theory of how they are generated. *Journal of Experimental Biology* 204:1333–1345.